Productive: Finding Joy in What We Do
Bible Studies for Life: Small Group Member Book

© 2013 LifeWay Press®

ISBN: 978-1-4300-2897-0

Item: 005602632

Dewey Decimal Classification Number: 248.84

Subject Heading: WORK \ LABOR PRODUCTIVITY \ REST

Eric Geiger
Vice President, Church Resources

Ronnie Floyd
General Editor

David Francis
Managing Editor

Gena Rogers
Karen Dockrey
Content Editors

Philip Nation
Director, Adult Ministry Publishing

Faith Whatley
Director, Adult Ministry

Send questions/comments to: Content Editor, *Bible Studies for Life: Adults*, One LifeWay Plaza, Nashville, TN 37234-0175; or make comments on the Web at *www.BibleStudiesforLife.com*.

Printed in the United States of America

For ordering or inquiries, visit *www.lifeway.com*; write LifeWay Small Groups; One LifeWay Plaza; Nashville, TN 37234-0152; or call toll free (800) 458-2772.

All Scripture quotations, unless otherwise indicated, are taken from the Holman Christian Standard Bible®, copyright 1999, 2000, 2002, 2003, 2009 by Holman Bible Publishers. Used by permission.

Bible Studies for Life: Adults often lists websites that may be helpful to our readers. Our staff verifies each site's usefulness and appropriateness prior to publication. However, website content changes quickly so we encourage you to approach all websites with caution. Make sure sites are still appropriate before sharing them with students, friends, and family.

Social Media

 Connect with a community of *Bible Studies for Life* users. Post responses to questions, share teaching ideas, and link to great blog content. ***Facebook.com/BibleStudiesForLife***

 Get instant updates about new articles, giveaways, and more. ***@BibleMeetsLife***

The App

Simple and straightforward, this elegantly designed iPhone app gives you all the content of the Small Group Member Book—plus a whole lot more—right at your fingertips. Available in the iTunes App Store; search **"Bible Studies for Life."**

Blog

At ***BibleStudiesForLife.com/blog*** you will find magazine articles and music downloads from LifeWay Worship. Plus, leaders and group members alike will benefit from the blog posts written for people in every life stage—singles, parents, boomers, and senior adults—as well as media clips, connections between our study topics, current events, and much more.

Work and rest. What's the biblical balance?

Balance.

Some people work too much. They trade relationships and fulfillment for experiences and stuff. Others barely do the minimum to stay employed and get a paycheck. They struggle to get by. Both groups need balance.

A joyous approach toward our work and a generous attitude toward our money are grounded in our relationship with Christ, lived out in community with others, and provide a refreshing witness to the culture around us.

This study lifts up the biblical mandates to work and to rest. It points us to actions that achieve balance. In light of these biblical values, we can move away from living and earning for ourselves and discover that our jobs, time, money, and life are resources we can invest for the kingdom of God.

Ronnie and Nick Floyd

Ronnie and Nick Floyd co-wrote this study. Ronnie has served as the Senior Pastor of Cross Church in Northwest Arkansas for more than 26 years. Nick Floyd, Ronnie's son, is one of the teaching pastors at Cross Church, preaching weekly at the Fayetteville campus.

This growing and innovative multi-site church is reaching thousands every week for Jesus Christ. Read Ronnie's blog at *RonnieFloyd.com*. Follow Ronnie and Nick on Twitter: *@RonnieFloyd* and *@NickFloyd8*.

contents

SESSION 1

GOOD WORK

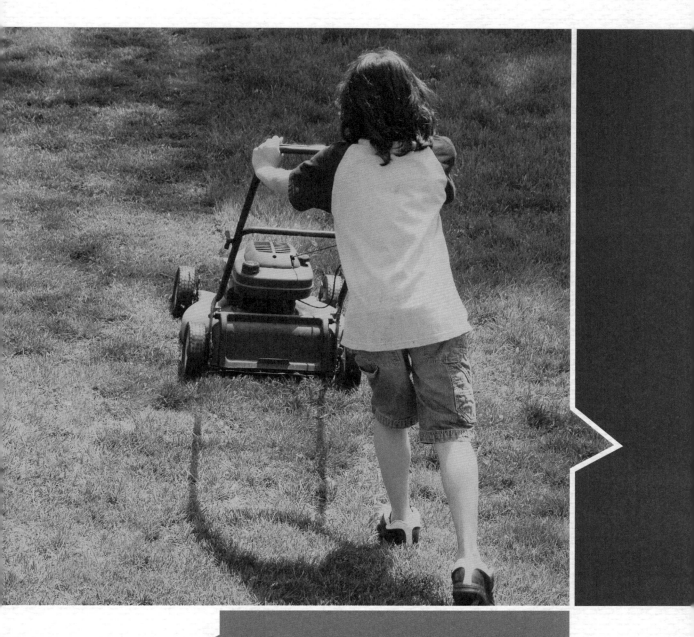

What did you like best about your first job?

Work is a gift from God, not a curse.

THE BIBLE MEETS LIFE

The bed is so warm and the room is so cold. Your eyes are heavy. You glance over at the alarm clock and feel the weight of a million problems and tasks waiting for you later in the day. You struggle out of bed, head blindly to the coffee pot, stumble into the shower, throw on your clothes, and head to work.

Some of us work all day just waiting for the shift to end so we can go home … and start the whole process over again. Day after day after day.

Is this really the work life that God intended us to have? No one is exempt from a tough day at work, but is our time working supposed to be one of misery and longing for the end of the day? In the Book of Genesis, God laid a very different foundation. In the first two chapters, God provided powerful words for how we are to approach our work.

WHAT DOES THE BIBLE SAY?

Genesis 1:28; 2:8-9,15-17 (HCSB)

1:28 God blessed them, and God said to them, "Be fruitful, multiply, fill the earth, and subdue it. Rule the fish of the sea, the birds of the sky, and every creature that crawls on the earth."

2:8 The Lord God planted a garden in Eden, in the east, and there He placed the man He had formed.

9 The Lord God caused to grow out of the ground every tree pleasing in appearance and good for food, including the tree of life in the middle of the garden, as well as the tree of the knowledge of good and evil.

15 The Lord God took the man and placed him in the garden of Eden to work it and watch over it.

16 And the Lord God commanded the man, "You are free to eat from any tree of the garden,

17 but you must not eat from the tree of the knowledge of good and evil, for on the day you eat from it, you will certainly die."

Key Words

garden (2:8)—This word comes from a Hebrew verb meaning "to defend" or "protect." In the garden in Eden, Adam and Eve experienced God's full protection and provision.

knowledge of good and evil (2:9)—Interpretations of this phrase vary but this is clear: this tree offered knowledge that was unnecessary, inappropriate, and forbidden for humanity. It led to shame, punishment, and expulsion.

Genesis 1:28

In Genesis 3:17-19, God placed a curse on our work as a result of Adam's disobedience. This curse affected our work, but work itself is not the curse. In fact, when we look at Genesis 1:28, we see that God ordained for Adam to be busy working. God gave Adam work *before* sin entered the picture.

God gave Adam three commands:

▶ **Reproduce:** Adam and Eve were to have children who would also reproduce and begin the process of filling the earth.

▶ **Bring order:** The picture here is one of subduing. This represents the responsibility for Adam and Eve to work faithfully to take advantage of the natural resources that God put around them.

▶ **Rule:** Adam and Eve were to have dominion over all the fish, birds, and every living thing. God established an order right from the beginning.

Since work is a gift from God and not a curse, we can see that God's plan in Genesis 1:28 is for us to be faithful in doing our work. God could've told them to sit idly by while waiting for Him to take care of all of their needs. Instead, God called Adam to be proactive.

One of the greatest ways we see work as a gift from God is the way God uses our jobs to provide for our families and those who depend on us. Without work, how would we meet those needs? Even in our moments of frustration with work, we can thank God for the provision that He brings through our work.

What is the relationship between God's blessing and our work?

QUESTION #2

How does your current work fulfill your purpose and advance God's kingdom?

QUESTION #3

Genesis 2:8-9,15

When we arrive at Genesis 2:8-9, we see two important factors in our understanding of work as a gift from God:

▶ God placed Adam and Eve in a specific location.

▶ God caused the land to flourish.

Think about this within the context of your own work. Understand two important principles.

1. **God places you in specific locations.** Think about where God has led you to work. Think about the education and experience that enabled you to get the job or do the work. Think about the relationships that were crucial in your hiring. Remind yourself that God has put together, piece by piece, every part of the picture of your life, including work.

2. **God blesses where He places you.** The garden was absolute perfection and unparalleled beauty. It provided a place for unbroken fellowship with God. God told Adam in chapter 1 to work the land. In chapter 2 God ordained trees to sprout up that would be beautiful for the eyes and full of fruit. Even though God gave Adam a task, it was still God who gave the blessing of growth.

How is your work a part of God's overall design?

QUESTION #4

Work is a gift from God, not a curse. Since that is true, we must learn to see ourselves in a good place where God pours out good things. He helps us earn a living, provide for our families, and enjoy His blessings while on this earth. God puts us in specific places—and blesses our lives at that place—to advance the kingdom of God. All the blessings we have received from God have not been accidents. Thus, we must use them for Him. Here's a key question to ask yourself: Why has God given me this particular work?

"We often miss opportunity because it's dressed in overalls and looks like work."

—THOMAS A. EDISON

> **What choices in your work will lead to blessing or curse?**
>
> QUESTION #5

Genesis 2:16-17

In the midst of the perfection of Eden, God told Adam not to eat of one tree. Everything else—the entire garden—was fair game. Instead of doing the work of the garden and enjoying the fruit God provided, Adam focused on the one thing he couldn't have. Consequently, he fell into sin. How often do we do that? God gives us work that provides for us and for the work of the kingdom. Yet we get sidetracked into sin. *"If I would've stuck with what God had called me to do, I never would've gotten myself into this mess!"*

▶ Adam had a choice between right and wrong.

▶ Adam had a choice between obedience and disobedience.

▶ Adam had a choice between a blessing and a curse.

We are also put in specific places by God to do what He has called us to do. We have choices:

▶ Will I show integrity?

▶ Will I cut corners?

How we make work choices shows what we believe about work. Sadly, many view work as a self-serving way to achieve status or accumulate things. Others view work as a sad reality to be endured. We must always be on guard against the enemy's tactics of causing discontent over what God has called us to do.

MODEL WORKER

Who taught you the value of work? Jot down characteristics about this person's attitude regarding work and what you learned.

LIVE IT OUT

So how do we choose to appreciate God's gift of work?

▶ **Guard against discontentment.** When you feel dissatisfied at work, mentally list at least three ways God has blessed you in your job.

▶ **Encourage a coworker.** Find a tangible way to encourage someone in his or her work. For example, leave a thank you note for the custodial crew. Give words of appreciation to the supervisor who led an excellent meeting.

▶ **Thank a mentor.** Recall the person you described in the page 13 activity. Write that person a note or message to express gratitude for teaching you how to work. Share in your note one or two key attributes that person modeled for you.

God uses work to teach us how to follow Him more deeply. **So hop out of bed, get the coffee going, and anticipate what God will do.**

Accept His Plan

Something seemed amiss ... I had been faithfully serving as a full-time music minister for 32 years. I loved my work. I was good at it. Though I had my share of struggles in church life, I had always imagined retiring as a full-time music minister.

That was not to be.

To continue reading "Accept His Plan" from *Mature Living* magazine, visit *BibleStudiesforLife.com/articles*.

My group's prayer requests

....

....

....

....

....

....

....

....

....

....

....

My thoughts

SESSION 2

WHO WE WORK FOR

What's the difference between a leader and a boss?

QUESTION #1   #BSFLwho

Work for Christ.

THE BIBLE MEETS LIFE

Maybe I wouldn't dread Mondays if I worked for someone else.

Another Monday. Another one of *those* meetings with *that* guy. You and your coworkers sit uncomfortably while getting berated like children. It seems every Monday brings another thought of a career change. Or at least the thought of your boss being reassigned to a company somewhere overseas.

Surely things would be better if someone else was in charge.

All of us have had a point in our careers when we have worked for someone who was not the greatest leader. And we've probably all entertained the thought of what we would tell that person if we ever mustered up the courage. We would unload on the person, then quit our job and walk out of the building free at last! More often than not, though, we wake up to reality and end up simply living in bitterness and longing for a better life. In the sixth chapter of Ephesians, God tells us how to handle situations like this. As believers, it is not about telling a person off, but about realizing whom we really work for.

WHAT DOES THE BIBLE SAY?

Ephesians 6:5-9 *(HCSB)*

5 Slaves, obey your human masters with fear and trembling, in the sincerity of your heart, as to Christ.

6 Don't work only while being watched, in order to please men, but as slaves of Christ, do God's will from your heart.

7 Serve with a good attitude, as to the Lord and not to men,

8 knowing that whatever good each one does, slave or free, he will receive this back from the Lord.

9 And masters, treat your slaves the same way, without threatening them, because you know that both their Master and yours is in heaven, and there is no favoritism with Him.

Key Words

Slaves (v. 5)—Can denote the lowest of slaves but is also the most frequent word for a servant. Here, Bible students generally associate this role with a contemporary employee.

masters (v. 5)—Most frequently translated "lord," this title refers to one having authority over another. In contemporary application, Bible students usually associate this role with an employer or supervisor.

a good attitude (v. 7)— Literally the compound word here is "well/good mind." It reflects the attitude of goodwill, kindliness, enthusiasm, or even affection or love.

Ephesians 6:5

Paul addressed the slaves who were in the church. This was not an approval of slavery. It was an encouragement about how to follow Jesus even if enslaved. Paul gave principles on how to work and how to view work. These apply to anyone who works for someone else, an employer, boss, or supervisor.

Isn't it interesting that the first thing Paul addressed is our own obedience toward those in authority over us? In tough work situations where a boss is not kind or fair, we still obey what he or she tells us to do.

> *How do you react to Paul's emphasis on obedience and fear?*
>
> QUESTION #2

As believers in Jesus Christ, we have one Master. Whether first-century slaves or 21st-century employees, bosses, or CEOs, we have one Master. He is Jesus Christ. Even so, while here on earth, we have people placed in authority over us. Paul told us to obey these earthly masters in two ways:

1. **Obey with fear and trembling.** This phrase indicates the respect we are to give those who are placed in authority over us. We are to honor them by actively obeying what they assign to us.

2. **Obey with a sincere heart.** We are to genuinely do the job. We don't try to take a shortcut or just get by. Obeying with sincerity means we choose to fulfill the requests of those above us.

The entire point of the passage hinges on the next few words. Paul told the Ephesians that they were to do their work "as to Christ" (v. 5). In other verses the point is phrased like this: "as slaves of Christ" (v. 6), "as to the Lord and not to men" (v. 7).

Paul instructed us to obey our earthly masters with fear and trembling and with sincerity of heart as if working for Jesus Himself!

> *How can you keep your heart engaged in work you don't particularly like?*
>
> QUESTION #3

Ephesians 6:6-8

Paul told us to work, and not only when people are watching. Have you ever tried to impress your boss in some way when he or she walked into the room? In the opposite way, has the phrase, "When the cat's away, the mice will play," ever described your week when your boss was on vacation? Paul addressed both scenarios in verse 6. He told us not to work to please others; instead, we are to do our work faithfully as slaves for Christ.

Verse 7 tells us to have a good attitude. This isn't angry agreement through clenched teeth to do what we're asked to do. It's sincerely responding well when given an assignment. Paul reinforced the main point by telling us again, "as to the Lord and not to men." How can we have a good attitude? By realizing we work for Christ and not for the person who asked us for that work.

Everything looks different in light of eternity—even work:

▶ When you respect your employers and others over you, God recognizes your obedience.

▶ When you work hard even while no one is watching, God sees.

▶ When you avoid the trap of being a people-pleaser to make yourself look better, God notices.

▶ When you respond with a good attitude toward those with authority over you, God recognizes it.

▶ When you work as if you are working for Christ, God is watching … and He rewards.

> *What does it look like practically to work for the Lord and not for people?*
>
> QUESTION #4

SINCE JESUS IS MY BOSS:

Choose one. How would this element of your work be different if you worked for Jesus Christ?

☐ How I treat coworkers

☐ How I act when my supervisor isn't watching

☐ How I value my work

Ephesians 6:9

Paul shifted in verse 9 to the master. The principles easily apply to how employers or bosses are to treat those who are under their authority. Paul's words remind us of Jesus' words in Matthew 7:12: "Whatever you want others to do for you, do also the same for them."

Do not lead by threatening. Some bosses believe threats and fear are the only way to get something done. Since these bosses believe people don't really want to work, they believe they must motivate through a fear of punishment, docked pay, or even termination. God shows us a different pattern. No one likes to be threatened. No one likes to feel like his or her job is on the line.

We all serve the same Master. Those in charge and those receiving the directions both answer to God. He does not play favorites. Perhaps at your workplace the boss favors certain people. They are the ultimate hard workers … but only while the boss is around. They drive everyone crazy. Maybe you feel the boss is deceived, simply because the favorites are good at office politics. Paul told us our Boss is different. God looks at the CEO in the same way that He looks at the entry level employee.

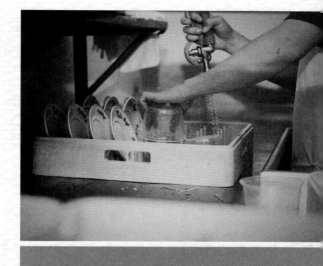

Paul wrote this to masters to remind them that they are no more special than the people who work under their authority. In leadership it is easy to think more highly of ourselves than we ought to. Paul makes it crystal clear that we better think twice before ever considering ourselves higher than the people who work for us. We all have the same Master. Humility and understanding are vital to good leadership.

> **What do we stand to gain by following Paul's instructions?**

QUESTION #5

LIVE IT OUT

What does Ephesians 6:5-9 prompt you to do at work?

▶ **Change your focus.** You ultimately work for Jesus Christ, so remind yourself of this by listing "Ephesians 6:7" or "Work for Christ" as the first task on your calendar.

▶ **Choose a godly attitude.** Even if your leaders are not fair or kind, you're responsible before God to act in a Christ-like manner toward them, toward work, and toward coworkers.

▶ **Start over.** Seek out your boss or coworkers and ask for forgiveness. Perhaps you've not worked in a way that represents Christ, or you've displayed attitudes and actions that should have been more Christ-like.

Mondays may still come too quickly, but you don't have to dread them anymore. **You truly are working for Someone Else— Jesus Christ.**

Labor Union

American Christians have a rather uneasy relationship with work. On Sunday, the lay person hears an impassioned message about sacrifice, self-denial, and the mission of God. He might be treated to a stirring testimony of a wealthy CEO who gave up a promising career to enter "full-time" ministry.

Then, Monday morning happens ...

To continue reading "Labor Union" from *HomeLife* magazine, visit *BibleStudiesforLife.com/articles*.

My group's prayer requests

....

....

....

....

....

....

....

....

....

....

....

My thoughts

SESSION 3

WHAT WE WORK FOR

What do you enjoy spending your money on?

QUESTION *#1*   #BSFLwhat

Support God's kingdom work with your income.

THE BIBLE MEETS LIFE

What do you work for? A new car? Clothes? Paying off debt?

According to the National Retail Association, in 2011, Americans spent 10.7 trillion dollars. Despite that figure, however, the world economy has challenged our circumstances—and our spending.

Some of us have lost jobs. Others have lost homes or savings. Perhaps we've lost a sense of security in the economy and the future. These losses cause us to ask: How can I save money to prepare for the future? How can I tighten my budget more than I already have? How can I fulfill the financial requests of groups, charities, and my church when it seems to take all I've got just to survive?

God has given us work and income to take care of our needs, but He does not give us money to use only for ourselves. As Christ-followers, we work so we can have resources to share with others. In Paul's Second Letter to the Corinthians, we discover how God has entrusted money and resources to us, so that we can support His work in the world today.

WHAT DOES THE BIBLE SAY?

2 Corinthians 8:1-9 (HCSB)

1 We want you to know, brothers, about the grace of God granted to the churches of Macedonia:

2 During a severe testing by affliction, their abundance of joy and their deep poverty overflowed into the wealth of their generosity.

3 I testify that, on their own, according to their ability and beyond their ability,

4 they begged us insistently for the privilege of sharing in the ministry to the saints,

5 and not just as we had hoped. Instead, they gave themselves especially to the Lord, then to us by God's will.

6 So we urged Titus that just as he had begun, so he should also complete this grace to you.

7 Now as you excel in everything—faith, speech, knowledge, and in all diligence, and in your love for us—excel also in this grace.

8 I am not saying this as a command. Rather, by means of the diligence of others, I am testing the genuineness of your love.

9 For you know the grace of our Lord Jesus Christ: Though He was rich, for your sake He became poor, so that by His poverty you might become rich.

Key Words

deep poverty (v. 2)—Poverty in Macedonia was severe. Among believers it was worse, made so by persecution for their faith. They were at rock bottom, destitute.

wealth (v. 2)—Despite their destitution, Macedonian believers gave with a remarkable depth of generosity. Here, "wealth" refers to the spirit and sacrifice with which they gave.

all diligence (v. 7)— Literally, "haste" or "speed." By implication, this means that which is done quickly or promptly, as with eagerness, zeal, diligence, or earnestness.

2 Corinthians 8:1-2

The apostle Paul called believers in Corinth to excel in all areas. He used churches in Macedonia as an example. Severe testing and trials pressed the Macedonians in ways unknown to the Corinthians. Their poverty was severe and they operated from rock-bottom destitution. Even through these problems, the Macedonians were known for their generosity.

These Christ-followers in Macedonia personally experienced the grace of God. They had come to a point of repenting of their sins and confessing Jesus as Lord and Savior. As they grew in faith, they learned that the same grace that saved them from the penalty of sin empowered them to live the Christian life. They discovered God's grace is so powerful it results in generosity to others and support for God's kingdom.

The believers in Macedonia gave from their spiritual wealth because of Jesus. They did not forget what He had done for them. As they experienced God's grace, they shared the grace of generosity with others. They were zealous to participate in giving opportunities. Grace was the power that ignited generosity.

▶ **Generosity is a lifestyle that gives freely.** When the grace of God makes us right with Jesus Christ, the condition of our heart changes.

▶ **A right heart results in open hands.** God who opened their hearts also opened their hands. Open hands represent the core understanding that God owns everything and we own nothing.

Whether our circumstances are productive or problematic, God's grace is the impetus for generosity. Generosity is a matter of the heart. When our heart is right with God, we will practice generosity.

Who is the most generous person you've known? Why?

QUESTION #2

2 Corinthians 8:3-7

Where is your heart in relation to 2 Corinthians 8:5? This verse shows the heart of the Macedonian Christians and churches: "Instead, they gave themselves especially to the Lord, then to us by God's will." On their own accord, they gave themselves to God and to God's people.

A right heart results in open hands. Giving to others, including supporting God's kingdom with your income, is a matter of the heart. Since generosity is a lifestyle in which you give freely and live openhandedly, this cannot be done without first giving yourself to the Lord. Notice the transition in verse 5. After giving their hearts first to God, they gave themselves to the people by God's will. How?

▶ **Willingly.** They gave voluntarily to God's work and His people. No one had to coerce or manipulate their giving. Their giving was not only according to their ability, but beyond their ability.

▶ **Sacrificially.** With all they had, they met the needs of others. These Christ-controlled followers committed to be a part of the ministry. They did not run from ministry; they ran to it.

▶ **Supremely.** While excelling in faith, speech, knowledge, diligence, and love, they were also being called to excel in giving. Paul called them to give supremely, not in a mediocre manner.

How do we give generously when finances are fixed or uncertain?

QUESTION **#3**

Which is easier to excel in: speech, knowledge, love, or financial generosity? Why?

QUESTION **#4**

MY GIVING SUPPORTS

> **All ministries in the church are needed, but which ones especially motivate you to give to your church? Why?**

MINISTRY

- ☐ Evangelism
- ☐ Student ministry
- ☐ Ministry to the needy
- ☐ Children's ministry
- ☐ Facilities and supplies (buildings, Bible study books, heat, AC, lights)
- ☐ Adult ministry
- ☐ Discipleship/ Bible study/ Small groups
- ☐ Women's ministry
- ☐ Singles' ministry
- ☐ Other:

REASON

"Generosity is impossible apart from our love of God and of His people. But with such love, generosity not only is possible but inevitable."

—JOHN MACARTHUR

2 Corinthians 8:8-9

In 1968, American Christians gave only 3.11 percent of their income to the church. By 2009, 41 years later, that percentage dropped to 2.38 percent! Some might blame the economy, the country, or circumstances beyond their control. But money spent on entertainment, pets, toys, technology, alcohol, and tobacco continues to escalate. Billions of dollars are wasted annually on things that have no eternal value.

The Macedonian Christians gave out of their poverty. Those in Corinth were blessed with more resources, but they had failed to finish the task of supporting the relief needed in Jerusalem. Paul called them to love God supremely and to show their love by giving supremely. The ultimate example of giving, though, was not the Macedonians. The highest example of giving was Jesus Christ, who gave up the riches of heaven so that we, who were poor and lost in sin, could become rich in Christ's forgiveness and love! Because Jesus loved us generously through His death on the cross, we should give generously.

▶ **Our giving is an appraisal of God's worth.** If we view God as sovereign and great, mighty to save, and generously loving us at all times, we tend to give more of our income to support God's kingdom. If we have a low view of God—seeing Him as our buddy or our servant—we give little to nothing.

▶ **When we have a high view of God, our giving to God's kingdom will be greater.** When we grasp the greatness of our God and we are in awe of His presence and holiness, we will give ourselves fully to Him. We will hold nothing back.

What can we change in our community if we, as a group, give generously?

QUESTION *#5*

LIVE IT OUT

In light of this session, how can you support God's kingdom?

▶ **Acknowledge that you're not the center of the universe.** Let your spending and giving be used for God's kingdom purposes, not for your own.

▶ **Re-prioritize your spending.** As part of the process of using your money for God's purposes some budget lines may need to move further up the priority list, and some move further down. For example, give up buying a new shirt so you can give that same money to support God's kingdom.

▶ **Tithe on Sunday.** Make this week's offering ten percent of this week's income.

God has given so much to you. He has entrusted resources to you. **Get caught up in the joy of spending for God's kingdom.**

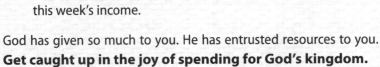

Spend Less, Give More

Like many Americans, you may be feeling bruised by the nation's economic problems and may be less inclined to stick with a giving plan. It can be tough to think about writing a check toward charitable causes when you're struggling to pay monthly bills and put food on the table. But regardless of your situation, here are some tips that can help jump-start your giving plan.

To continue reading "Spend Less, Give More" from *HomeLife* magazine, visit *BibleStudiesforLife.com/articles*.

My group's prayer requests

_____
_____
_____
_____
_____
_____
_____
_____
_____
_____
_____

My thoughts

SESSION 4

PUT YOUR MONEY TO WORK

What's the toughest part about budgeting?

QUESTION #1

#BSFLmoney

Be ready to give as the need arises.

THE BIBLE MEETS LIFE

Show me your bank statement and I will show you your priorities.

How do we determine what's important and what's not so important? Groceries, medical expenses, insurance, housing, car expenses, clothing, and the list goes on. Are any of these not important? Feeding the family? Important. Reliable transportation? Important. Each category needed in our budget has value, but how we spend and how much we spend in those categories can speak volumes.

For most of us, creating a budget is not fun. And living within its restraints can seem even less fun. But budgeting frees us to consider one other valuable category: meeting the needs of others.

What does our spending say about the importance of giving to meet the needs of others? The Bible calls us into a wise plan for giving, a course of action that can make us all better stewards of our money.

WHAT DOES THE BIBLE SAY?

2 Corinthians 8:10-15; 9:1-5 *(HCSB)*

8:10 Now I am giving an opinion on this because it is profitable for you, who a year ago began not only to do something but also to desire it.

11 But now finish the task as well, that just as there was eagerness to desire it, so there may also be a completion from what you have.

12 For if the eagerness is there, it is acceptable according to what one has, not according to what he does not have.

13 It is not that there may be relief for others and hardship for you, but it is a question of equality—

14 at the present time your surplus is available for their need, so their abundance may also become available for our need, so there may be equality.

15 As it has been written: The person who gathered much did not have too much, and the person who gathered little did not have too little.

9:1 Now concerning the ministry to the saints, it is unnecessary for me to write to you.

2 For I know your eagerness, and I brag about you to the Macedonians: "Achaia has been prepared since last year," and your zeal has stirred up most of them.

3 But I sent the brothers so our boasting about you in the matter would not prove empty, and so you would be prepared just as I said.

4 For if any Macedonians come with me and find you unprepared, we, not to mention you, would be embarrassed in that situation.

5 Therefore I considered it necessary to urge the brothers to go on ahead to you and arrange in advance the generous gift you promised, so that it will be ready as a gift and not as an extortion.

Key Words

equality (v. 13)—Paul encouraged Corinthian believers to share with needy Christians in Jerusalem out of a sense of equality with them. Then all would have what they needed.

boasting (v. 3)—Boasting or bragging can be good or bad. In verse 3, Paul used the term in commending the Corinthians' initial readiness to give.

extortion (v. 5)—This term can also be translated "grudgingly given," "exaction," or "covetousness." Paul was not pressuring but encouraging them to willingly give (9:7) what they had promised earlier.

> **Why is it hard to be generous over the long haul?**

2 Corinthians 8:10-11

Relief was needed in Jerusalem and an offering was being taken to provide that relief. A year earlier, the Corinthian believers had promised to give this help, yet the task had not been completed. Therefore, Paul encouraged them to complete their commitment, as the Macedonian believers had done.

In the United States we are blessed with the greatest military force in the world. While many things make the men and women who serve our nation special, I believe their readiness to serve is what sets them apart. They are always ready to go wherever they are needed and do whatever is necessary to defend our nation. Likewise, when needs arise around us, we should be ready to give.

Notice the honesty of Paul's appeal in these verses:

▶ **"I am giving an opinion."** Paul was not acting as God, but opened his heart and spoke to the people about all of this.

▶ **"It is profitable for you."** It would be to the Corinthians' advantage to participate in this offering.

▶ **"Finish the task."** This gospel endeavor was worthy. The need was credible. It was time to finish what they had started. We don't know if the people were distracted, if life had sidelined them, or what. Now was the time to finish what they had committed to do. Their integrity was on the line.

Surely, as followers of Jesus Christ, we should profess our readiness not only with words, but also with actions. Readiness begins with an attitude, but always involves an action.

What principles about healthy giving did
Paul communicate in this passage?

QUESTION #3

2 Corinthians 8:12-15

Extremes abound. On one end of the giving spectrum we hear the appeals of those who promote a prosperity gospel. They advocate that if people commit by faith to give something, whether they have it or not, God will provide more for them to give. They say you can give your way into the prosperity of this world.

At another end of the spectrum we hear a call for Christians to give away everything they have. These teachers claim poverty is the way of life for Christ-followers.

How are we to understand what is right? God's Word is very clear:

▶ **Give according to what you have, not what you don't.** Christians are to give by the standard of what God has entrusted to them. Jesus said: "Much will be required of everyone who has been given much. And even more will be expected of the one who has been entrusted with more" (Luke 12:48). As God has blessed us in life, we should step up to the level of God's blessings! We may desire to give $1 million to a need; but cannot give this amount if our salary is $30,000 annually and our total net assets are less than $50,000. On the other hand, we never should desire to give only $10 to a major need if we earn a six figure income!

▶ **It is a matter of equality.** This passage is not an appeal to redistribute wealth. The apostle Paul taught those in Corinth to give while they were enjoying surplus and were able to give. A time might come later when the Corinthians would be the ones in need. Therefore we all choose to be generous and help. The people we help may be the ones who help us later.

Love leads us to be generous. And generosity always desires to meet the needs of others.

If you had a financial need that was met by a group of
believers, what would that communicate to you?

QUESTION #4

WHERE DOES IT ALL GO?

Create a pie chart to show where your money generally goes each month (housing, food, transportation, insurance, and so on).

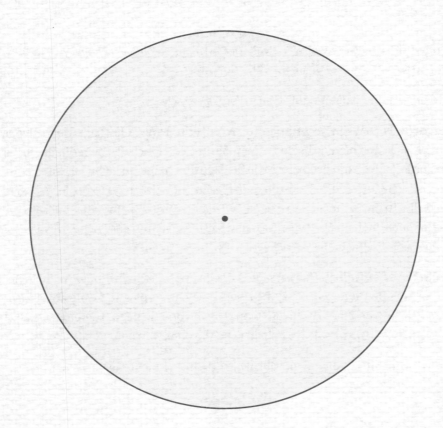

My Monthly Spending

Where does giving to the needs of others fall?

2 Corinthians 9:1-5

What steps can we take now so we can give when a need arises?

QUESTION #5

One year earlier, Paul had received an incredible report from the Christians in Corinth. They pledged to give relief to Christians in Jerusalem—and they promised to give generously. Their zeal and eagerness was genuine. Paul boasted of their generosity to the Macedonian believers. This inspired the Macedonians to give generously—and they did not have nearly the wealth the Corinthians had.

Nearly a year later, Paul used the Macedonians' generosity to inspire the Corinthians to follow through. Paul sent Titus to Corinth to arrange for their generous gift. We find specific takeaways in these verses:

▶ **Eagerness is contagious.** Zeal inspires others. When we want to inspire, we do not enlist someone halfway committed to make the appeal. We choose someone who eagerly obeys God.

▶ **Nothing is wrong with asking people to make a financial commitment to give.** The apostle Paul was very clear in what he was asking from the Corinthians.

▶ **Accountability is acceptable.** Paul sent Titus to ensure the Corinthians followed through on their commitment to give. Without accountability, greed and stealing from God can occur.

▶ **Giving is not about getting.** Genuine, generous giving expects nothing in return.

Our motives for giving are very important to God, and to people. Be ready to give as the need arises, but do so with the right motives.

"A bone to the dog is not charity. Charity is the bone shared with the dog, when you are just as hungry as the dog."

—JACK LONDON

LIVE IT OUT

What will it take for you to be ready to give as the need arises?

▶ **Take a step toward the generous side.** Give a financial gift to ministry efforts through your church. Ask God how much to give.

▶ **Spend less.** Review your receipts to see where you spend your money. (Recall the pie chart on page 42.) What can you adjust to have money to give, both for now and for later?

▶ **Volunteer in a ministry that assists those facing financial struggles.** Commit to pray for someone you meet there.

God wants you to put whatever resources you have to work for Him. He did not give you money to hoard or waste, but to use to meet needs. **Align your priorities with God's and be ready to give as the need arises.**

Budget Crunch

Our family has recently lived through a season of change. We've experienced changes in careers, changes in lifestyle, changes in education ... and most importantly, changes in our hearts.

To continue reading "Budget Crunch" from *HomeLife* magazine, visit *BibleStudiesforLife.com/articles*.

My group's prayer requests

_____

_____

_____

_____

_____

_____

_____

_____

_____

_____

My thoughts

SESSION 5

WORK YOUR PLAN

When have you recently seen a demonstration of generosity?

QUESTION #1

#BSFLplan

Generous giving should glorify God and reflect Christ's giving.

THE BIBLE MEETS LIFE

In 2009, Bill and Melinda Gates, along with Warren Buffett, began to dream about how they could use their massive wealth for the good of others. The next year they launched the Giving Pledge (*GivingPledge.org*) to challenge the world's billionaires to give at least half their net worth to charity. Their challenge was to do this during their lifetime, through a legacy, or in a combination of both.

You might be thinking, *"Well, sure, if I were a billionaire, I would easily give away half of my wealth!"* Think so? The reality is that if we are not in the habit of giving when we have little, we probably won't give when we have more.

While we applaud the generosity of others, let's consider our own level of giving. We noted in session three that in 2009, American Christians only gave an average of 2.38 percent of their income to their church (see p. 33). The Bible, however, calls us to a different standard. God's Word not only calls Christ-followers to give, but we are called to give with great generosity.

WHAT DOES THE BIBLE SAY?

2 Corinthians 9:6-13 (HCSB)

6 Remember this: The person who sows sparingly will also reap sparingly, and the person who sows generously will also reap generously.

7 Each person should do as he has decided in his heart—not reluctantly or out of necessity, for God loves a cheerful giver.

8 And God is able to make every grace overflow to you, so that in every way, always having everything you need, you may excel in every good work.

9 As it is written: He scattered; He gave to the poor; His righteousness endures forever.

10 Now the One who provides seed for the sower and bread for food will provide and multiply your seed and increase the harvest of your righteousness.

11 You will be enriched in every way for all generosity, which produces thanksgiving to God through us.

12 For the ministry of this service is not only supplying the needs of the saints, but is also overflowing in many acts of thanksgiving to God.

13 They will glorify God for your obedience to the confession of the gospel of Christ, and for your generosity in sharing with them and with others through the proof provided by this service.

Key Words

reluctantly (v. 7)—Genuine Christian benevolence is defined by the attitude of the giver. To give reluctantly (literally, "out of sadness or sorrow," thus "grudgingly") is not pleasing to the Lord.

cheerful (v. 7)—Giving with a cheerful attitude delights the Lord. This Greek word is behind the English *hilarious*. It describes an attitude of happy compliance or cooperation. Christian giving is a blessing, not a burden.

2 Corinthians 9:6-7

Paul challenged the Christians in Corinth to give generously to the offering being received for the believers suffering in Jerusalem. The principle of sowing and reaping is not only an agricultural principle, but also a giving principle. Notice the freedom and joy that follow giving.

▶ **The level of your investment will determine the level of your return.** Just as a farmer who plants a little seed will harvest a small crop, the giver who gives a little will receive a limited blessing. Conversely, if a farmer plants much seed, he will harvest a large crop.

▶ **God loves a "hilarious" giver.** The word translated "cheerful" comes from the Greek *hilaros*, from which we get our term *hilarious*. Giving generously should be fun, provide joy as we do it, and flow through us with the utmost enthusiasm.

> *When have you gotten a thrill out of giving generously?*
>
> QUESTION #2

2 Corinthians 9:8-9

Because God is powerful and mighty He is able to:

▶ Make every grace overflow to you

▶ Ensure that you have everything you need

▶ Enable you to excel in every good work

Generosity is a lifestyle. Generous givers don't hold on to their resources or rewards. Why? Generous givers understand that God owns everything and we are managers of God's blessings in this life.

You cannot out-give God. When you are willing to circulate His blessings and share them with others, God will circulate more blessings for you to share.

> *Is this passage more about resources, trust, or ownership? Explain.*
>
> QUESTION #3

2 Corinthians 9:10-11

God will produce more than we need. Does that mean we will get rich if we give? Some isolate verse 10 to teach this. They interpret the verse to mean that if we give generously, God will make us rich. Some claim God wants all His children to live in nicer homes, drive luxurious cars, take fabulous vacations, and so on.

The idea that serving the Lord will make you rich is not new. Paul wrote to Timothy about "people whose minds are depraved and deprived of the truth, who imagine that godliness is a way to material gain" (1 Tim. 6:5).

Rather than embrace giving as a way to financial prosperity, study verses 10-11 to see how generous giving glorifies God and demonstrates the gospel:

▶ God is the One who provides necessities of life and more. He is the One who will multiply our material resources.

▶ The reason for multiplying our material resources is to increase the harvest of our righteousness. That involves meeting physical and spiritual needs of others in Jesus' name.

▶ God prospers us not so we can move on up and enjoy a bigger piece of the pie, but to enable us to do more to bless others. Paul stressed again the ministry of giving. The point is that material wealth is never the point. The point is to "seek first the kingdom of God and His righteousness;" we then trust Him to provide life's necessities (Matt. 6:33).

▶ Our generosity will result in people offering thanksgiving to God, thus bringing glory to Him.

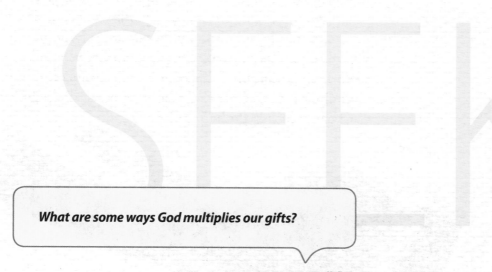

What are some ways God multiplies our gifts?

QUESTION *#4*

2 Corinthians 9:12-13

What does generosity do?

> ▶ **Generosity supplies the needs of the saints.** When followers of Jesus Christ are willing to live like their Lord, giving freely and living openhandedly, then the needs of the saints are met. When the Christians in Jerusalem received this offering from their fellow Christians in Corinth, their needs were met.

> ▶ **Generosity expresses thanks to God.** A generous heart is a thankful heart. And a thankful heart is a generous heart. When we are actively and acutely aware that God has given us everything we have, we are expressing thanks to God. When we know that our resources are not just for our own enjoyment, but we are to share them with others, we are expressing thanks to God. Giving is a tangible way God has given us to express our love to Him.

> ▶ **Generosity confesses the gospel of Jesus Christ to everyone.** Through our generosity to others, we confess that Jesus is first in our lives and we are to testify to the world that we belong to Him. Jesus Christ generously gave Himself for us; as we accept His free gift of life, He brings us into right standing before God. We belong to Jesus and we are to imitate Him through expressing generosity to others. Generosity is diametrically opposed to our tendency to be selfish. Generosity demonstrates our allegiance to King Jesus and the kingdom of God.

How does your generous giving communicate the gospel of Jesus Christ?

QUESTION #5

IT ALL ADDS UP

Choose 1 or 2 statements to complete.
I can be more generous by:

☐ cutting back on . . .

....

....

☐ ordering the smaller . . .

....

....

☐ skipping the extra . . .

....

....

☐ earning more money by . . .

....

....

☐ selling . . .

....

....

LIVE IT OUT

Where do you go from here?

▶ **Put some money aside.** A little money saved regularly means you'll have money to purchase supplies for a mission trip, contribute to the ramp that makes your church accessible to more people, and otherwise reach people for Christ.

▶ **Raise your percentage.** Raise the percentage of your giving by at least one percent. Over time keep raising your percentage as God guides you to do so.

▶ **Draw up a will, or revise the will you have, to leave a portion to a Christian ministry.** This is one of many ways to leave a legacy, to reach people for Jesus even after you go on to heaven.

It doesn't take a billionaire to change the world. It just takes a love for Jesus. **Show your love for Jesus through generosity.**

Hungry to Help

It doesn't add up. Every year the world produces enough food so that each person can eat 2,700 calories a day. And yet, at this very moment, 925 million people in the world are hungry. Today as is true every day, nearly 16,000 children will die from hunger-related causes.

To continue reading "Hungry to Help" from *HomeLife* magazine, visit *BibleStudiesforLife.com/articles*.

My group's prayer requests

_____
_____
_____
_____
_____
_____
_____
_____
_____
_____

My thoughts

SESSION 6

GIVE WORK A REST

How would you describe
a truly restful day?

Rest is a gift from God for His glory and your benefit.

THE BIBLE MEETS LIFE

The "E" is bright red. The needle is falling further and further. Whether you'll make the next mile or not is anyone's guess. This could be you on the freeway, but what if it were your day-to-day life? Do you ever feel like your tank is on empty?

Life can be brutal at times: five days or more at work, games on the weekends with the kids, the grind, the money, the stress.

One of the hardest things to do in the midst of work and life is to intentionally take time to hit the brakes and rest. While God desires us to work hard, He also desires us to rest hard.

What did God do on the seventh day of creation? He rested. Does God need rest? No. But God set a precedent for how our lives are supposed to work. In the Book of Exodus we see this principle reiterated. In this session we can learn to work hard and rest with intentionality.

WHAT DOES THE BIBLE SAY?

Exodus 31:12-17 *(HCSB)*

12 The LORD said to Moses:

13 "Tell the Israelites: You must observe My Sabbaths, for it is a sign between Me and you throughout your generations, so that you will know that I am Yahweh who sets you apart.

14 Observe the Sabbath, for it is holy to you. Whoever profanes it must be put to death. If anyone does work on it, that person must be cut off from his people.

15 Work may be done for six days, but on the seventh day there must be a Sabbath of complete rest, dedicated to the LORD. Anyone who does work on the Sabbath day must be put to death.

16 The Israelites must observe the Sabbath, celebrating it throughout their generations as a perpetual covenant.

17 It is a sign forever between Me and the Israelites, for in six days the LORD made the heavens and the earth, but on the seventh day He rested and was refreshed."

Key Words

Sabbaths (v. 13)—Sabbath means "rest." For the Israelites, the last day of every week (thus the plural Sabbaths) was to be a holy Sabbath, set apart from other days in that work was forbidden.

profanes (v. 14)—To belittle or defile the Sabbath by treating it as just another day is to profane it or desecrate it.

Exodus 31:12-13

By observing a day of rest you bring glory to God. God told Moses this one action of observing the Sabbath day would be a sign to all generations that God was the One who had sanctified Israel. It was God Himself who had made the difference in the lives of these people. In many ways, this was an upward or vertical principle, meaning it displayed the relationship between God and His people.

Ancient Israel had none of our modern conveniences. Think of the agricultural nature of that time in history and the daily work such responsibilities would have required. Even in the midst of the work and the grind of this era of history, God commanded people to stop, to pause, and to remember.

An entire group of people, one day every week, rested completely. And we are called to do the same.

▶ We do not observe the Sabbath in the same way the Israelites did, but the principle from creation spans across all periods of history.

▶ Our observance of the principle of rest still stands today, not because it is rooted in Jewish tradition, but it is rooted in the act of creation.

▶ Because of this fact, we celebrate the Lord's Day as a day to worship our Savior and rest from work. Our observance of a day of rest is countercultural. It is a shining sign to the world that we have been saved by Jesus. It is Jesus who has sanctified and set us apart.

God also wants us to rest for our own benefit. Work hard for six days, then rest. Are you worn out? Are you constantly bouncing from activity to activity every day and night of the week and weekend? Could it be that you are not observing God's principle of worship and rest?

> *How is a Sabbath rest different from and similar to other types of rest?*

QUESTION #2

How does God's view of the Sabbath differ from our culture's view?

QUESTION #3

Exodus 31:14-15

The Sabbath day was not just any other day. This was a day to tangibly remember what God had done for them. It was a day to pause and reflect on the great works of God.

In Exodus 31:14-15, we see the consequence for failing to observe the Sabbath: death. If anyone did any work whatsoever, they were to be put to death. This penalty shows how important it was to God that His people obey this command. This day was to be a holy day. To not observe the Sabbath was to profane the God who lovingly calls His people to rest.

▶ **The Sabbath is a solemn rest.** When we think of solemn events, a level of seriousness and quietness comes to mind. There's an overall respect for whatever event is taking place. Think about a time when we have had a national tragedy. Even if you are at a sporting event sandwiched between crazed fans, a moment of silence is often observed to commemorate and pray for the victims of the tragedy. This is a great picture of the Sabbath. In the middle of our busy lives, we are to pause with a level of seriousness and honor. We do this on the day God calls us to rest.

▶ **The Sabbath is holy.** God declared this day is to be a holy day. This is not like the rest of the week. This is not like another normal day of work. This is a special day. It's a day to honor. It's a day to live differently and to be different.

What comes to mind when you think of the word "holy"? Whatever it is, it is most likely something out of the ordinary. Something is special and honorable about it. God told His people to make the Sabbath a day like that.

> **What does this command tell us about God's design for our relationship with Him?**
>
> QUESTION #4

Exodus 31:16-17

God tied observing the Sabbath to the covenant between Himself and His people. The Sabbath was put into place to display the relationship between God and His people. You may have a group of friends from church, work, or your college days. You get together with this group periodically, maybe gathering in a central location once a month or once a year. Why? The relationships. When you do a regular tradition or ritual like this, you show the value of the relationship and of doing something to strengthen it.

The word "covenant" is often used in discussions about marriage. In the covenant of marriage, two people agree before God to live their lives together. We use items to symbolize the marriage covenant such as wedding rings. Each spouse wears a band as a sign that they are in a covenant relationship.

A Sabbath rest is a symbol, a public display of devotion to our Lord. We belong to God and to one another.

In verse 17, God again connected the Sabbath rest to creation. While some may connect the Sabbath rest exclusively to the Old Testament, the connection to creation shows us this is a pattern for all believers at all times. Our motivation for rest is obedience. Our goal is to be like God.

Work hard—that's the entire point of this study. God has designed us for work and has given us this blessing. But a vital part of God's model for work is rest. God uses this day of rest and worship to refresh, recharge, and push us forward for the next week.

> **What boundaries can we put in place to help us keep a Sabbath rest?**
>
> QUESTION #5

PLAN MY SABBATH REST

This refreshes/relaxes me:

This leads me to worship/ reflect upon God:

How I can make these a weekly part of my Sabbath rest:

"Solitude well practiced will break the power of busyness, haste, isolation, and loneliness."

—DALLAS WILLARD

LIVE IT OUT

How can you put the principles of rest and worship into practice?

▶ **Schedule your Sabbath.** Make Sabbath rest part of your weekly plan. Keep it just like any other appointment.

▶ **Get everyone on the same page.** Schedule a family meeting. Agree together what you will do each week to take a day for rest and worship.

▶ **Implement necessary changes.** Identify responsibilities from which you need to rest for one day to experience a Sabbath. Identify actions that will help you rest and reflect. Review the activity on page 63 for ideas.

It's time to hit the brakes and fill up the tank. Follow God's example, and **give work a rest.**

A sanctuary in Time

Speeding through life at what I believed was a healthy pace, I ran out of gas without as much as a flicker from the fuel warning light. I completed projects and checked off to-do lists without hesitation until I woke up one Monday feeling like a ghost of my former self, hollow and faintly present.

A quick self-inventory suggested something deep down inside was broken.

To continue reading "A Sanctuary in Time" from *HomeLife* magazine, visit *BibleStudiesforLife.com/articles*.

My group's prayer requests

....

....

....

....

....

....

....

....

....

....

....

My thoughts

Productive: Finding Joy in What We Do

For the past six weeks, we have been challenged and encouraged to take a different look at how we work and how we use our money. A joyous approach toward our work and a generous attitude toward our money are grounded in our relationship with Christ, lived out in community with others, and provide a refreshing witness to the culture around us.

Christ

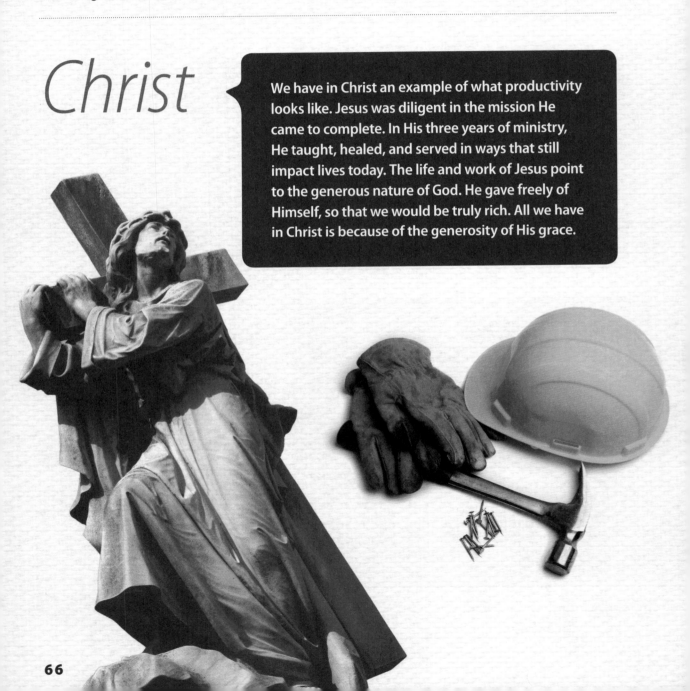

We have in Christ an example of what productivity looks like. Jesus was diligent in the mission He came to complete. In His three years of ministry, He taught, healed, and served in ways that still impact lives today. The life and work of Jesus point to the generous nature of God. He gave freely of Himself, so that we would be truly rich. All we have in Christ is because of the generosity of His grace.

Community

Generosity is carried out in the context of community. The act of giving should connect us to the ones we seek to help. Whether we are the ones giving or the ones receiving, humble generosity without condescension brings us together. The community of believers helps one another.

Culture

The world teaches us to earn a lot so that we can have a lot. God's Word teaches a different approach: earn so that you can invest in others. Our productivity in the workforce is tied to more than a paycheck; how we carry out our work and what we do with what we earn speak volumes about what is truly important to us. When our work is done to honor Christ, our teaching about Christ becomes attractive (Titus 2:10). Productivity does more than produce widgets; it produces changed lives.

LEADER GUIDE

PRODUCTIVE

GENERAL INSTRUCTIONS

In order to make the most of this study and to ensure a richer group experience, it's recommended that all group participants read through the teaching and discussion content in full before each group meeting. As a leader, it is also a good idea for you to be familiar with this content and prepared to summarize it for your group members as you move through the material each week.

Each session of the Bible study is made up of three sections:

1. THE BIBLE MEETS LIFE.

An introduction to the theme of the session and its connection to everyday life, along with a brief overview of the primary Scripture text. This section also includes an icebreaker question or activity.

2. WHAT DOES THE BIBLE SAY?

This comprises the bulk of each session and includes the primary Scripture text along with explanations for key words and ideas within that text. This section also includes most of the content designed to produce and maintain discussion within the group.

3. LIVE IT OUT.

The final section focuses on application, using bulleted summary statements to answer the question, *So what?* As the leader, be prepared to challenge the group to apply what they learned during the discussion by transforming it into action throughout the week.

For group leaders, the *Productive* Leader Guide contains several features and tools designed to help you lead participants through the material provided.

QUESTION 1—ICEBREAKER

These opening questions and/or activities are designed to help participants transition into the study and begin engaging the primary themes to be discussed. Be sure everyone has a chance to speak, but maintain a low-pressure environment.

DISCUSSION QUESTIONS

Each "What Does the Bible Say?" section features at least three questions designed to spark discussion and interaction within your group. These questions encourage critical thinking, so be sure to allow a period of silence for participants to process the question and form an answer.

The *Productive* Leader Guide also contains follow-up questions and optional activities that may be helpful to your group, if time permits.

DVD CONTENT

Each video features teaching from Ronnie and Nick Floyd on the primary themes found in the session. We recommend that you show this video in one of three places: (1) At the beginning of group time, (2) After the icebreaker, or (3) After a quick review and/or summary of "What Does the Bible Say?" A video summary is included as well. You may choose to use this summary as background preparation to help you guide the group.

The Leader Guide contains additional questions to help unpack the video and transition into the discussion. For a digital Leader Guide with commentary, see the "Leader Tools" folder on the DVD-ROM in your Leader Kit.

SESSION ONE: GOOD WORK

The Point: Work is a gift from God, not a curse.

The Passage: Genesis 1:28; 2:8-9,15-17

The Setting: Genesis 1 tells us of God's work of creation. Genesis 2 focuses on one aspect of that creation: His creation of man, the culmination of His creation. God placed Adam in the garden of Eden. In the midst of this perfect setting, Adam was given the assignment to work the garden and watch over it. With that task came the freedom to enjoy the garden and the fruit of his work.

QUESTION 1: What did you like best about your first job?

> *Optional activity:* Bring to the group meeting several printouts of current job openings. These could come from the classified section of a newspaper or from career websites such as *www.monster.com*. (Be creative about which jobs you choose to print, but also be sensitive to the current situations of your group members.) Pass the printouts around for a few minutes, then ask the following questions:
>
> - What surprised you about any of these job opportunities?
> - *Which of these jobs would you be most likely to apply for? Why?*

Video Summary: In this first video message, Nick Floyd emphasizes the point of this week's session—work is a gift from God, not a curse. There is a common misconception that work is a result of the fall when, in fact, God put in place a plan for work before the fall occurred. Genesis 1:28 and 2:15 both illustrate God's plan for Adam—to reproduce, bring order, and rule in the garden. God placed Adam and Eve in a specific place for a specific purpose. And in the same way, wherever we work, whatever we do, God has placed us there sovereignly.

WATCH THE DVD SEGMENT FOR SESSION 1, THEN USE THE FOLLOWING QUESTIONS AND DISCUSSION POINTS TO TRANSITION INTO THE STUDY.

- Nick talks about how Adam and Eve chose to disobey God and that decision changed the course of history, even our work. Work is not a result of the fall, but the fall absolutely affected our work. In what ways have you seen this to be true in your own life?
- What are some ways you can live out the truth that "work is good" in your own job? Be specific.

WHAT DOES THE BIBLE SAY?

ASK FOR A VOLUNTEER TO READ ALOUD GENESIS 1:28; 2:8-9,15-17.
Response: What's your initial reaction to these verses?

- What do you like about the text?
- What questions do you have about these verses?

TURN THE GROUP'S ATTENTION TO GENESIS 1:28.
QUESTION 2: What is the relationship between God's blessing and our work?

The passage states that God blessed Adam and Eve in a specific way that includes the "work" of subduing the earth. This interpretation question asks the group to articulate this relationship in their own words.

> *Optional follow-up:* What's the difference between work and a job?

MOVE TO GENESIS 2:8-9,15.

QUESTION 3: How does your current work fulfill your purpose and advance God's kingdom?

Continuing the thread from the prior question, this asks group members to apply their response to the first question by making it more personal. This is an application question.

> ***Optional follow-up:*** What are some ways you work to advance God's kingdom that don't involve your "day job"?

QUESTION 4: How is your work a part of God's overall design?

Self-revelatory in nature, this question takes the group discussion deeper into the hearts and minds of each group member. Ultimately this asks the group to look for ways to make their work more God-honoring.

CONTINUE WITH GENESIS 2:16-17.

QUESTION 5: What choices in your work will lead to blessing or curse?

This question challenges the group to consider specific actions and how each leads to blessing or curse. For instance, a group member may answer that stopping gossip or complaining at work can lead to a better attitude. Another may commit to early morning prayer and Scripture reading to make her time at work more effective.

> ***Optional follow-up:*** What steps can you take to be more intentional about recognizing those choices when they arise?

> ***Optional activity:*** Direct participants to complete the "Model Worker" activity on page 13 of the group member book. Invite volunteers to share their responses with the group.

Note: The following question does not appear in the group member book. Use it in your group discussion as time allows.

QUESTION 6: What advice would you give to someone whose work feels like a curse?

This question directs you back to the point of the lesson. It's an opportunity to put the truth of Genesis 1:28 to work in our relationships. Group members must first internalize this truth before they can impart it to others.

LIVE IT OUT

Invite group members to consider these three ways to appreciate God's gift of work:

- **Guard against discontentment.** When you feel dissatisfied at work, mentally list at least three ways God has blessed you in your job.
- **Encourage a coworker.** Find a tangible way to encourage someone in his or her work. For example, leave a thank you note for the custodial crew. Give words of appreciation to the supervisor who led an excellent meeting.
- **Thank a mentor.** Recall the person you described in the page 13 activity. Write that person a note or message to express gratitude for teaching you how to work. Share in your note one or two key attributes that person modeled for you.

Challenge: Your career is a gift from God that is a means of His provision both for you personally and for His kingdom. Spend some time this week identifying ways God uses your work to help you financially and spiritually. Consider how He might use your work and work relationships to benefit others.

Pray: Ask for prayer requests and ask group members to pray for the different requests as intercessors. As the leader, close this time by committing the members of your group to the Lord and asking Him to help each of you remember and live out of the truth that your work is a gift from God.

SESSION TWO: WHO WE WORK FOR

The Point: Work for Christ.

The Passage: Ephesians 6:5-9

The Setting: In Ephesians 5, Paul gave the command to be filled with the Holy Spirit and began showing how submission and reverence are to be carried out in our relationships. Paul addressed family relationships—husbands, wives, and children—before turning to work relationships. Paul addressed both slaves and masters, grounding every aspect of their work under the lordship of Christ.

QUESTION 1: What's the difference between a leader and a boss?

> *Optional activity:* Ask for pairs of volunteers to role-play the following situations as a way of exploring what it looks like to work for Christ. In each case, designate one volunteer as the boss and the other as the employee.
>
> • The boss is asking the employee to manipulate expense reports in order to hide purchases from upper management.
>
> • The boss knows the employee has lied about being sick for several days because the employee has posted pictures and commentary of a recent vacation on Facebook. The boss has decided to confront the employee.
>
> • The boss is confiding sensitive information to the employee about other coworkers. The employee feels uncomfortable with the situation and decides to confront the boss.

Video Summary: In this week's video message Nick passes on a reminder about who it is we really work for. Ephesians 6:5-9 tells us that as believers, we work for Christ. We are to respect those in authority over us and serve them out of the sincerity of genuine, pure hearts, but ultimately it is not those people we work for. In this passage Paul reminds us of our ultimate goal in working—to do the will of God. In Ephesians 6:9 he speaks directly to masters/bosses, admonishing them as well. No matter our rank or position, we all have the same God and there is no partiality with Him.

WATCH THE DVD SEGMENT FOR SESSION 2, THEN USE THE FOLLOWING QUESTIONS AND DISCUSSION POINTS TO TRANSITION INTO THE STUDY.

> • Share with the group a time when you had difficulty serving a boss with respect and sincerity. How were you able to work through that situation?
>
> • Did anything from Nick's message change the way you view your relationship with your employer and/or employees? Explain.

WHAT DOES THE BIBLE SAY?

ASK FOR A VOLUNTEER TO READ ALOUD EPHESIANS 6:5-9.
Response: What's your initial reaction to these verses?

- What questions do you have about these verses?
- What application do you hope to gain about how you are to work and relate to those you work for?

TURN THE GROUP'S ATTENTION TO EPHESIANS 6:5
QUESTION 2: How do you react to Paul's emphasis on obedience and fear?

This question is included to provide an opportunity for the group to discuss how the Bible meets life in Ephesians 6:5. Scripture encourages us to work out our faith (Philippians 2:12) and this question creates an environment for such work. Consult the commentary on the DVD-ROM for additional support.

Optional follow-up: How does our culture view the kind of obedience and fear Paul emphasized in these verses?

MOVE TO EPHESIANS 6:6-8.
QUESTION 3: How can you keep your heart engaged in work you don't particularly like?

Answering this question is crucial to living the kind of productive life described in the Bible. Most likely you'll find several people who struggle with keeping their hearts engaged in their work. Be prepared with your own answer.

QUESTION 4: What does it look like practically to work for the Lord and not for people?

This is an application question. Encourage the group to cite specific actions that can be taken to work for the Lord only—not for people.

Optional activity: If you have access to a whiteboard or large sheet of paper, ask a volunteer to make a list of what it looks like to work for the Lord and a second list of what it looks like to work for people.

Optional activity: Direct participants to complete the activity "Since Jesus is My Boss" on page 22 of the group member book. Invite volunteers to share their responses.

CONTINUE WITH EPHESIANS 6:9.
QUESTION 5: What do we stand to gain by following Paul's instructions?

Purely an interpretation question, this question points group members back to the passage to examine it for the ways we're blessed through the kind of obedience described in Ephesians 6:5-9.

Optional follow-up: What do we stand to lose?

Optional follow-up: How have you experienced these gains and losses in your own life?

Note: The following question does not appear in the group member book. Use it in your group discussion as time allows.

QUESTION 6: What obstacles are preventing or hindering your ability to work for Christ right now?

Ending the group time by identifying road blocks allows group members to leave with a working knowledge of things that stand between them and working for Christ. You might want to follow up on this question next week.

LIVE IT OUT

Direct group members to consider these three things that Ephesians 6:5-9 prompts them to do at work:

- **Change your focus.** You ultimately work for Jesus Christ, so remind yourself of this by listing "Ephesians 6:7" or "Work for Christ" as the first task on your calendar.

- **Choose a godly attitude.** Even if your leaders are not fair or kind, you're responsible before God to act in a Christ-like manner toward them, toward work, and toward coworkers.

- **Start over.** Seek out your boss or coworkers and ask for forgiveness. Perhaps you've not worked in a way that represents Christ, or you've displayed attitudes and actions that should have been more Christ-like.

Challenge: God knows exactly what He is doing in your work. He is working in your life to accomplish His purposes. Many times He uses things within our work lives to teach us how to follow Him in a deeper way. Spend some time this week thinking of instances in your life when you have seen this to be true. Consider journaling about those experiences so you can reread them the next time you need a reminder.

Pray: Ask for prayer requests and ask group members to pray for the different requests as intercessors. As the leader, close this time by committing the members of your group to the Lord and asking Him to help each of you approach your work in a way that is pleasing to God.

SESSION THREE: WHAT WE WORK FOR

The Point: Support God's kingdom work with your income.

The Passage: 2 Corinthians 8:1-9

The Setting: The churches in Macedonia had been collecting an offering to help with the needs of the poverty-stricken believers in Jerusalem. The church at Corinth was to participate in this offering, but Paul needed to encourage them to follow through with their gift. He used the example of the Macedonian churches, who gave out of their poverty, to challenge the Corinthians to excel in the grace of giving.

QUESTION 1: What do you enjoy spending your money on?

Optional activity: Work as a group to come up with a list of three or four ideas for group mission trips and service projects. When finished, discuss the following questions as a group for each item on the list:

- What would it realistically cost to make this happen for our group?
- How could we adjust this idea to get the most "ministry bang" for our buck?

Video Summary: This week's video message reminds us of the importance of knowing what we are working for. God has entrusted us with money and resources to support Him, His work, and others. In 2 Corinthians 8:1-5 the apostle Paul calls believers in Corinth to excel in all areas of life, and he uses the Macedonians as examples. Even through trials, they became known for their generosity. But they didn't practice generosity out of their monetary wealth. Instead it was an overflow of their spiritual wealth. They gave willingly, voluntarily, and sacrificially. Just as with the Macedonians, it is God's grace that empowers and ignites our generosity.

WATCH THE DVD SEGMENT FOR SESSION 3, THEN USE THE FOLLOWING QUESTIONS AND DISCUSSION POINTS TO TRANSITION INTO THE STUDY.

- "Giving is a matter of the heart." Where is your heart today?
- How might the concept of giving out of your spiritual wealth rather than your monetary wealth change the way you view your role in supporting God's kingdom work?

WHAT DOES THE BIBLE SAY?

ASK FOR A VOLUNTEER TO READ ALOUD 2 CORINTHIANS 8:1-9.

Response: What's your initial reaction to these verses?

- What questions do you have about these verses?
- What new application do you hope to get from this passage?

TURN THE GROUP'S ATTENTION TO 2 CORINTHIANS 8:1-2.

QUESTION 2: Who is the most generous person you've known? Why?

By identifying a specific person, each group member will define his or her own notions of generosity and what makes a person generous.

Optional follow-up: Generosity is a common term in Scripture and society; what does it really mean to be generous?

MOVE TO 2 CORINTHIANS 8:3-7.

QUESTION 3: How do we give generously when finances are fixed or uncertain?

This is an application question. Remind the group that it's not about "if" but about "how."

Optional follow-up: How do we identify the line between being prudent and being stingy?

QUESTION 4: Which is easier to excel in: speech, knowledge, love, or financial generosity? Why?

This is an interpretation question that asks the group to look more closely at 2 Corinthians 8:3-7 and consider what they may hold most dear. Often it's the things we cling to most desperately that reveal the enemy's strongholds.

Optional follow-up: Which of these four do you find most challenging to excel in? Why?

Optional activity: Ask group members to complete the activity "My Giving Supports" on page 32 of the group member book. Ask volunteers to share the areas where they are most motivated to give and why.

CONTINUE WITH 2 CORINTHIANS 8:8-9.

QUESTION 5: What can we change in our community if we, as a group, give generously?

This question asks the group to visualize a world of generosity and how each member may contribute to it.

Optional activity: You may want to start by reviewing and/or adjusting the trips and service projects you identified in the opening optional activity.

Note: The following question does not appear in the group member book. Use it in your group discussion as time allows.

QUESTION 6: What are some of your dreams and/or goals when it comes to giving generously?

This is an opportunity for group members to tell stories of dreams and goals they may have. Encourage sharing.

LIVE IT OUT

Direct group members to three ways they can support God's kingdom:

- **Acknowledge that you're not the center of the universe.** Let your spending and giving be used for God's kingdom purposes, not for your own.

- **Re-prioritize your spending.** As part of the process of using your money for God's purposes, some budget lines may need to move further up the priority list and some move further down. For example, give up buying a new shirt so you can give that same money to support God's kingdom.

- **Tithe on Sunday.** Make this week's offering 10 percent of this week's income.

Challenge: God has given you much. He has entrusted it to you freely and generously in order for you to give it back to Him and His work. This week think of some new areas where you can give generously to God's kingdom.

Pray: Ask for prayer requests and ask group members to pray for the different requests as intercessors. As the leader, close this time by asking the Lord to help each of you find opportunities to share your resources with others.

SESSION FOUR: PUT YOUR MONEY TO WORK

The Point: Be ready to give as the need arises.

The Passage: 2 Corinthians 8:10-15; 9:1-5

The Setting: As we learned from the previous session on 2 Corinthians 8, the churches in Macedonia had been collecting an offering to help with the needs of the poverty-stricken believers in Jerusalem. As Paul wrote to encourage the Corinthians to follow through with their gift, he called them to give in proportion to the way God had blessed them. Instead of rebuking the church, Paul used the positive example of the churches of Macedonia to spur the Corinthians to give as they had planned.

QUESTION 1: What's the toughest part about budgeting?

> *Optional activity:* Bring a bag of candy to the group—anything that contains at least several dozen pieces. To help group members start thinking about crunching numbers and solving problems, open the bag and instruct the group to divide the candy evenly among participants.
>
> - Materials: 1 bag of candy; you may also want to bring paper bowls for dividing the candy.
> - It's likely the candy won't divide evenly. Simply task them with identifying a "fair" solution. When they finish, guide them to make connections between this decision and living within a budget.

Video Summary: This week Ronnie talks about putting the money God has given us to work. The point of this session is that we need to be ready to give as the need arises. Second Corinthians 8:10-11 serves as a reminder that we don't want to miss what God wants to do in our lives as well as the lives of others through our money. In this passage Paul challenges the Corinthians to follow through and live a lifestyle of true generosity—a lifestyle in which they give freely and live openhandedly. Generosity always desires to meet the needs of others.

WATCH THE DVD SEGMENT FOR SESSION 4, THEN USE THE FOLLOWING QUESTIONS AND DISCUSSION POINTS TO TRANSITION INTO THE STUDY.

- Both 2 Corinthians 8:12-15 and Luke 12:48 speak to giving according to what you have, not what you do not have. In what ways does this message relieve some of the pressure related to giving that you may have felt in the past?

- What will it take for you to be ready to give as the need arises?

WHAT DOES THE BIBLE SAY?

ASK FOR A VOLUNTEER TO 2 CORINTHIANS 8:10-15; 9:1-5.
Response: What's your initial reaction to these verses?

- What do you like about the text?

- What new application do you hope to receive about being ready to share your resources?

TURN THE GROUP'S ATTENTION TO 2 CORINTHIANS 8:10-11.
QUESTION 2: Why is it hard to be generous over the long haul?

This is a question that requires some authenticity, honesty, and transparency—all attributes of effective group life. Giving over the long haul is a mark of spiritual maturity to which all believers should aspire. Encourage the group toward a posture of generosity as opposed to a case-by-case approach.

MOVE TO 2 CORINTHIANS 8:12-15.
QUESTION 3: What principles about healthy giving did Paul communicate in this passage?

Point the group to the text. This is an observation question included here to reiterate the principles found in this passage about being generous.

Optional follow-up: What are some other Bible passages or stories that teach about healthy giving?

QUESTION 4: If you had a financial need that was met by a group of believers, what would that communicate to you?

To consider how this might impact us personally helps us better understand how others are affected when we step out to meet a financial need in their lives.

Optional follow-up: When have you been blessed by the generosity of others?

Optional follow-up: What emotions do you experience when you receive kindness and/or generosity from others? Why?

Optional activity: Ask participants to complete the activity "Where Does It All Go?" on page 42 of the group member book. Ask for volunteers to share where their money goes each month.

CONTINUE WITH 2 CORINTHIANS 9:1-5.

QUESTION 5: What steps can we take now so we can give when a need arises?

This question helps group members put together action steps. Challenge the group to talk specifically (e.g. trade in the gas guzzling SUV, give up the club membership, etc.).

> ***Optional follow-up:*** What obstacles often prevent us from taking these kinds of steps?

> ***Optional follow-up:*** How can these obstacles be overcome?

Note: The following question does not appear in the group member book. Use it in your group discussion as time allows.

QUESTION 6: Why do you think God wants His people to give money to others? (What's the ultimate goal of giving generously?)

This question asks group members to consider what they really think about God and Who He is to them. Answers will vary, but giving generously is good for us. God wants what is best not only for others, but also for us.

LIVE IT OUT

Encourage group members to consider these three things they can do to be ready to give as the need arises:

- **Take a step toward the generous side.** Give a financial gift to ministry efforts through your church. Ask God how much to give.

- **Spend less.** Review your receipts to see where you spend your money. (Recall the pie chart on page 42.) What can you adjust to have money to give, both for now and for later?

- **Volunteer in a ministry that assists those facing financial struggles.** Commit to pray for someone you meet there.

Challenge: God wants you to put whatever resources you have to work for Him. Spend some time this week examining your heart. Consider why you may not be living as the generous person God wants you to be.

Pray: Ask for prayer requests and ask group members to pray for the different requests as intercessors. As the leader, close this time by asking the Lord to help each of you see the things that are keeping you from being able to freely give as the need arises.

SESSION FIVE: WORK YOUR PLAN

The Point: Generous giving should glorify God and reflect Christ's giving.

The Passage: 2 Corinthians 9:6-13

The Setting: We continue our study from 2 Corinthians 8–9, where Paul addressed the issue of an offering that was being collected for the benefit of suffering believers in Jerusalem. Paul reminded the church at Corinth that the principle of sowing and reaping applies to giving. The Corinthians could be free and generous, knowing that God would use their gift and provide for them.

QUESTION 1: When have you recently seen a demonstration of generosity?

> *Optional activity:* Bring several of the following objects to the group meeting and display them where all participants can see. (Feel free to bring in other objects that fit the theme, as well.) Ask group members to choose the object they feel best represents the concept of giving generously and to explain their choice. Objects: spade, bucket, wallet or purse, clock, gift bag, checkbook, battery, spark plug, and so on.

Video Summary: This week Ronnie talks about working our plan. Second Corinthians 9:6-7 tells us that the level of our investment will determine the level of our return. The passage also reminds us that God loves a cheerful and generous giver. Generosity is a lifestyle that allows us to give freely and live openhandedly. When our hearts are right, our hands are open. God intends for us to live generously and trust Him with the outcome.

WATCH THE DVD SEGMENT FOR SESSION 5, THEN USE THE FOLLOWING QUESTIONS AND DISCUSSION POINTS TO TRANSITION INTO THE STUDY.

- How would you assess your own generosity?
- In his message, Ronnie talks a lot about acting now. What practical steps can you take this week to move forward with your plan?

WHAT DOES THE BIBLE SAY?

ASK FOR A VOLUNTEER TO READ ALOUD 2 CORINTHIANS 9:6-13.

Response: What's your initial reaction to these verses?

- What questions do you have about these verses?
- What new application do you hope to get from this passage?

TURN THE GROUP'S ATTENTION TO 2 CORINTHIANS 9:6-7.

QUESTION 2: When have you gotten a thrill out of giving generously?

This is an opportunity for sharing and storytelling. Encourage this aspect of group life.

> *Optional follow-up:* What it is about giving that you find fun? Why?

> *Optional follow-up:* What obstacles can take the joy out of giving?

MOVE TO 2 CORINTHIANS 9:8-9.

QUESTION 3: Is this passage more about resources, trust, or ownership? Explain.

Generally there are 4 types of questions: observation, interpretation, application, and self-revelation. This is an interpretation question that asks each group member to offer his or her own interpretation of the text.

CONTINUE WITH 2 CORINTHIANS 9:10-11.

QUESTION 4: What are some ways God multiplies our gifts?

This question is included so group members can see God's creativity in multiplying our gifts. It requires specific examples. Be prepared to share your own.

> *Optional follow-up:* When have you experienced one of these ways in your life?

CONTINUE WITH 2 CORINTHIANS 9:12-13.

QUESTION 5: How does your generous giving communicate the gospel of Jesus Christ?

The gospel of Jesus Christ is central to the life of any believer. This question asks group members to connect their giving with the gospel.

> ***Optional follow-up using Luke 16:1-13:*** Is it appropriate to use money and other forms of generosity as a seed for proclaiming the gospel? Explain.

> ***Optional activity:*** Ask group members to complete the active "It All Adds Up" on page 53 of the group member book. Ask for volunteers to share their responses of ways they can be more generous.

Note: The following question does not appear in the group member book. Use it in your group discussion as time allows.

QUESTION 6: What's the difference between "generous giving" and normal giving?

Without making the routine giver feel like he or she is missing something, encourage the group to compare and contrast a posture of generosity that is dynamic and attentive with a more rote or routine giving that is perhaps stale and uninspired.

LIVE IT OUT

Encourage group members to consider these options for where they can go from here:

- **Put some money aside.** A little money saved regularly means you'll have money to purchase supplies for a mission trip, contribute to the ramp that makes your church accessible to more people, and otherwise reach people for Christ.

- **Raise your percentage.** Raise the percentage of your giving by at least one percent. Over time keep raising your percentage as God guides you to do so.

- **Draw up a will, or revise the will you have, to leave a portion to a Christian ministry.** This is one of many ways to leave a legacy, to reach people for Jesus even after you go on to heaven.

Challenge: Take some time this week to reflect on these questions. Consider journaling your responses. And be willing to push past yes or no answers: Do you give freely and live openhandedly? Do you give joyfully and enthusiastically?

Pray: Ask for prayer requests and ask group members to pray for the different requests as intercessors. As the leader, close this time by asking the Lord to help each of you give generously.

SESSION SIX: GIVE WORK A REST

The Point: Rest is a gift from God for His glory and your benefit.

The Passage: Exodus 31:12-17

The Setting: On Mount Sinai, God gave Moses the Ten Commandments, which included the command to remember and keep the Sabbath (Exodus 20:8-11). In the chapters that followed, God gave further laws— ceremonial, judicial, and moral laws—and in that law He reiterated the importance and value of keep the Sabbath as a holy day of rest and celebration. The Sabbath rest served as a sign to the Israelites to lead them to remember who God is and their covenant relationship with Him.

QUESTION 1: How would you describe a truly restful day?

> ***Optional activity:*** Help group members experience a mini-Sabbath by declaring five minutes of rest at the beginning of your group meeting. Tell group members they can do anything they find restful—nap, play games, talk, eat, and so on. When the five minutes are over, use the following questions to unpack the experience.
>
> - What did you choose as your form of rest? Why?
> - How do you feel after resting?
> - Do you find it easy or difficult to build rest into your daily routine? Your weekly routine?

Video Summary: In this last session, Nick talks about how rest is a gift from God for His glory and our benefit. In the Exodus 31 passage God sends Moses to tell the Israelites to take a break. We also see in this chapter that God modeled this rest He intended for the Israelites. He created for six days and then He rested. But this principle of a Sabbath is for us as well. In the midst of hard work and stress, God says, "Come and rest." When we do this, it's a sign of our relationship with the Lord—a sign that we have been changed by Him.

WATCH THE DVD SEGMENT FOR SESSION 6, THEN USE THE FOLLOWING QUESTIONS AND DISCUSSION POINTS TO TRANSITION INTO THE STUDY.

- We are called to work hard. When was the last time you felt completely worn out and exhausted?
- We are also called to rest hard. When was the last time you truly observed a day of rest and worship?

WHAT DOES THE BIBLE SAY?

ASK FOR A VOLUNTEER TO READ ALOUD EXODUS 31:12-17.
Response: What's your initial reaction to these verses?

- What questions do you have about resting the way the Lord intends?
- What new application do you hope to get from this passage?

TURN THE GROUP'S ATTENTION TO EXODUS 31:12-13.
QUESTION 2: How is a Sabbath rest different from and similar to other types of rest?

This question asks group members to define what the Sabbath is to them—what it is and what it isn't. Don't shy away from discussion about the meaning and application of true rest.

> ***Optional follow-up:*** Is the Sabbath limited to a specific day of the week? Explain.

MOVE TO EXODUS 31:14-15.
QUESTION 3: How does God's view of the Sabbath differ from our culture's view?

Point the group to the text. This question asks the group to consider how their understanding and definition of rest from the prior question is colored by the culture's definition.

> ***Optional follow-up:*** Why is it noteworthy that God labeled the Sabbath as "holy"?